11.90
10%

DATE DUE

AUG 4 – 1992	JAN 1 5 2005	
OCT 1 5 1993	JAN 1 7 2005	
OCT 1 8 1993	OCT 0 7 2006	
NOV – 9 1994		
DEC 2 1 1995		
NOV 2 1 1996	JAN 2 7 2010	
MAR 2 9 1997	NOV 2 9 2011	
OCT 2 3 1997	APR 0 9 2012	
FEB 2 4 1998	APR 2 1 2014	
SEP 1 1 1998		
AUG 1 7 1999	JUL 2 0 2015	
	JAN 1 4 2016	
FEB 1 4 2000		
MAR 0 8 REC'D		
OCT 1 6 2000		
MAR 1 1 2002		

Chemistry

Contents

Chemistry

1

Ancient Ideas

Some five thousand years ago in the Near East, a man was preparing to make an axe head. He had found the material for it that morning in a dry riverbed in the nearby desert—a piece of twisty brown rock shaped, oddly enough, somewhat like a twig from a tree. As the man knew, this was a very special kind of rock.

He made a fire in a shallow pit in his workplace, which was a sandy courtyard near his dwelling. The pit was filled with glowing coals, and in the center of them he placed a clay pot into which he put the chunk of rock. Then he squatted and began blowing steadily on the coals through a hollow reed. This, he knew, would make them burn much hotter, although he didn't know why. He also knew that the heat would make the pot and the rock in it hotter and hotter until, suddenly, the rock would dissolve into a thick, shimmering reddish-gold liquid. The man did not know why this should happen, either. But he would pour the liquid into a clay mold, and when it cooled it would be a smooth, shiny, sharp axe head, as hard as the stone had been. Without knowing the reasons for most of the things he did, he was using chemistry to change a lump of copper into a useful tool.

Chemistry is the science of the substances that make up everything in the universe—the study of their characteristics (hardness, softness, odor, etc.), how they act under different conditions, and what happens to them when they are mixed together in different combinations. Chemistry has always affected people's lives, and does so today more than ever. It plays an enormous part in producing many of the foods we eat, the clothes we wear, and scores and scores of the things we use and do every day. Our general knowledge of chemistry, such as understanding why things rust, why they burn, how they are formed, and so on, affects the way we think about our world and universe. But all the knowledge of chemistry that makes so many things possible today was completely unknown for thousands of years. Much of that knowledge was discovered only some two hundred years ago, by one man who literally created the science of chemistry as it is known today, and thus helped build our modern world.

EARLY SCIENTISTS

Back in prehistoric times, people were using chemistry for such things as making metal tools and weapons, glass, pottery, and paints and dyes. But they had no idea why the things they did worked, or why certain substances behaved as they did under certain conditions. They used fire for many purposes, but no one had the least idea what fire *was*, or what was happening when something burned. And no one had much of an idea of how substances were formed. Some people thought everything had formed from water.

Some ancient Greek scholars, the scientists of the ancient world, thought about these things. Two of them, named Leucippus and Democritus, suggested that everything was formed from countless tiny, hard particles of various sizes and shapes. They believed that these particles must be the very smallest objects that existed, and that they were indestructible—in other words, they couldn't be destroyed or even divided into smaller particles. Democritus named these things *atoms*, from a Greek word that meant "uncuttable."

Another Greek scholar, Empedocles, who lived at about the same time as Leucippus and Democritus, had a different idea. He believed that everything was made out of combinations of four basic substances that he called "the roots of things." These substances were earth, air, fire, and water. He thought up some pretty good proofs for this idea. For example, if a young, green branch was cut off a tree, droplets of water could be seen at the cut end, and this seemed to prove that one of the things that formed wood was water. The branch would burn, of course, and Empedocles said this showed

The Greek scholar
Empedocles (top), and
a woodcut illustrating,
clockwise from top,
fire, air, earth,
and water, which he
believed were "the
roots of things."

that it contained fire. As it burned it gave off smoke, which Empedocles believed was a form of the element air, and when it was completely burned, the gray ash that was left, which resembled dust and soil, was supposedly the earth that had formed part of the wood. About a century later, one of the greatest of Greek scholars, Aristotle, improved on Empedocles' idea and gave the four substances the name *elements*. Most other early scholars agreed with this idea of four basic elements.

THE EGYPTIAN ART

Shortly after Aristotle's time the land of Egypt was conquered by the Greeks and ruled by Greek kings. The ideas of the Greek scholars such as Aristotle became part of the Egyptian culture or way of life, and Greek scientific ideas began to flourish there. And so about 2,200 years ago, Egyptian scholars, many of whom were part Greek, began to study seriously the way different substances behaved. They heated them, burned them, mixed them together, and performed many other experiments. The Egyptians called this study of substances *chemaia*, from which comes our word *chemistry*. In ancient times, Egypt was known by the name *Khem* or *Khemia*, so the word *chemaia* may have meant something like "the Egyptian art."

The Egyptian chemists completely accepted the idea that all things were formed out of different combinations of the elements earth, air, fire, and water. And some of them soon began to think that

*The Greek scholar Aristotle from a painting
by Raphael. Aristotle was the first to name
earth, air, fire, and water as "elements."*

if they could just somehow rearrange the elements of a substance, they could change it into something else. What most of them hoped to do was turn a "common" metal such as lead or tin into a precious metal such as gold or silver! For hundreds of years, the main goal of most ancient chemists was to produce artificial gold. In their attempts to do this they burned, boiled, baked, melted, and mixed together almost every substance they could think of, in every way they could think of. They *calcined* solid substances by roasting them until they turned to powder; they *fused* substances by melting them together so that they were thoroughly mixed when they cooled and became solid; they *sublimated* solids by heating them until they gave off gases which turned into liquids when they cooled; and they *distilled* liquids in the same way. No one ever discovered how to make artificial gold, of course, but these early chemists did discover the ways that many substances could be changed by different processes. In the course of doing all this they invented many kinds of furnaces, melting pots, and equipment for fusing, sublimating, and distilling. Some of their inventions are used, without change, to this day.

Although the ancient chemists learned and accomplished many useful things, what they did included a great deal of magic, astrology, and superstition. They believed, for example, that each kind of metal was related to a planet or star—gold to the sun, silver to the moon, and so on. They called minerals and chemicals by magical-sounding names like "Seed of the Dragon" and "Water of the

Moon." For most of these people, the attempt to try to turn a "base" (low quality) metal, such as tin or lead, into the "noble" (high quality) metal gold was almost a kind of holy work. They felt that if they were successful they would become pure and noble beings—greater and more worthwhile than ordinary people!

The Egyptian study of chemistry reached its height in A.D. 200–300. By that time, Egypt was part of the immense and powerful Roman Empire. Rome maintained law and order, peace and prosperity, and a high regard for education and knowledge throughout the lands it ruled. The Egyptian city of Alexandria boasted the finest university and library in the empire, and it was in Alexandria where most chemists lived and worked, and where the books many of them had written were stored.

Between the 300s and 400s the Roman Empire began to come apart because of civil wars, religious conflicts, and invasions by barbarian tribes. Law and order began to break down throughout the empire. In the year 415 a terrible riot caused the closing of the university in Alexandria. The study of chemistry, as well as most other areas of learning, came to a stop.

In 476 the empire fell apart completely. Italy and other parts of Europe that had formed the western portion of the empire were split into many tiny kingdoms that began fighting among themselves. The eastern part of the empire, centered in what is now part of Turkey, was still supposedly in charge of Egypt, but it was busy fighting off inva-

The great library at Alexandria, Egypt,
was a haven for chemists and their books.
The library was built at the beginning
of the third century B.C. and destroyed
in a civil war six hundred years later.

sions of the barbarian Huns and attacks of the powerful Persian Empire. Then, in 639, the Muslims came sweeping out of Arabia bent on conquering the world, and Egypt became part of *their* new empire.

ALCHEMISTS
OF ARABIA

During the time since the collapse of the Roman Empire there had been little if any law and order in Egypt, and little chance for education and study. But the Muslim Empire established peace, law and order, and a regard for education that was as great as it had been under the Romans. Arab scholars discovered the books that had been written by Egyptian chemists of previous centuries, and the study of chemistry started up again. However, the Arabs tacked their word *al*, or "the," onto the old name *chemaia*, and called their study of substances *alchemy*.

Most of the Muslim alchemists accepted without question all the statements and ideas they read in the old books, believing that the Egyptian chemists had actually done and proved all the things they had written about. Thus, the Muslim alchemists believed in the four elements—earth, air, fire, and water, in *transmutation* (changing one substance into another), as well as all the magic and mumbo-jumbo. But they also began adding a lot of ideas of their own, and some of their ideas were destined to play a part in chemistry for hundreds of years.

One of the Muslim alchemists whose ideas became a major force in alchemy was an Arab known as Jabir ibn Hayan, who lived in the 700s. Jabir believed that the four elements possessed "qualities" of hotness, coldness, dryness, and wetness, and it was the mixture of these qualities that gave different substances their form. Thus, sulfur, a dry yellow powder that burns easily, was formed of the qualities dryness and hotness, or earth and fire, according to Jabir. Mercury, also called quicksilver (the thick, silvery liquid in medical thermometers), was formed of coldness and wetness; air and water. Jabir worked out the idea that it was combinations of sulfur and mercury in the earth that formed all the different kinds of metals. The kind of metal that was formed depended upon the pureness of the sulfur and mercury, and Jabir believed that if they were perfectly pure, the metal formed would be gold.

Jabir reasoned that if you could somehow completely purify quantities of sulfur and mercury, you could mix them together and make gold. He decided that this purification could be done by means of what he called an *al-iksar*, meaning (in Arabic) "dry material" — in other words, a sort of magic powder. To try to make this powder, Jabir burned, baked, melted, and mixed various kinds of minerals as well as blood, bones, hair, mustard, pepper, and a great many other things. He is credited with having written several books presenting all his ideas, which were widely accepted by other Muslim alchemists who were soon also trying to make an *al-iksar* with which they could produce gold.

Jabir ibn Hayan (721–776), an Arab chemist, based his ideas on the belief that the elements earth, air, fire, and water possessed the qualities of dryness, coldness, hotness, and wetness.

Although it may seem that Jabir and the other Muslim alchemists were simply dabbling with nonsense, that's not quite correct. Jabir based his ideas on a great deal of careful thought and some actual experiments. He was really doing the best he could with the knowledge of chemistry available at his time — which was not very great. He was actually a good chemist for his day, and his books contained a lot of information on the chemical processes involved in making such things as nitric acid, acetic acid, varnish, and a number of other useful things.

In time, the books by Jabir and some of the other Muslim alchemists were brought to Europe and fell into the hands of people who could translate them. Europeans became aware of this study of substances; they, too, called it *alchemy*, because that was what the Arabs called it.

2

The Alchemists of Europe—
Magic, Mystery, and Trickery

The study of alchemy in Europe began in the 1100s, during the period that we now call the High Middle Ages, or Medieval period. There were, of course, many European people *using* chemistry at this time — metalsmiths, cloth dyers, glassmakers, and so on — but the idea of studying chemical processes to find out what made them happen, or of experimenting with different substances to find out about them, just hadn't occurred to anyone except perhaps a very few scholars. Unlike the Muslim Empire, where things were fairly quiet and education and scholarship were encouraged, life in much of Europe was constantly being interrupted by warfare, and there was little if any time or thought given to learning. Most of the barons, dukes, and even kings could not read or write, and there were no schools or universities in most of Europe until well into the 1100s. Only in the monasteries, where priests and

monks lived away from the rest of the world, were education and learning fostered.

Europe had been pretty well cut off from the Near East for centuries because of religious differences and warfare, and few Europeans knew much about what was going on there. But the Muslims had conquered Spain in 718, and it had been under their influence for centuries. The study of alchemy was as widespread in Spain as in the rest of the Muslim Empire, and the few European scholars outside of Spain who knew about alchemy (mostly priests) learned about alchemy from visits to Spain and contacts with Spanish scholars. The first book on alchemy to appear in Europe, in the year 1144, was an Arabian work translated by an English priest studying in Spain. Most of the first Europeans to study alchemy were monks and priests, because they were among the only people with enough education to be able to read and translate the books of Muslim alchemists. In time, some priests, such as the English Franciscan Roger Bacon, began to write their own books on alchemy, in European languages. By that time, there were universities run by the Church in many major European cities, and more

Most of the first Europeans to study alchemy were monks and priests. Shown here is the English monk Roger Bacon (1214–1294) in his observatory on top of the tower of the cloister at Oxford.

people in other walks of life, such as doctors, were able to read. The study of alchemy began to flourish.

THE PHILOSOPHER'S STONE

Just as the Arab scholars had unquestioningly believed everything they read in the books by the Egyptian chemists, so did most Europeans at first believe everything they read in the books written by Arabs and other Muslims. So in Europe, too, people now began to look for ways to transmute one of the "base" metals into "noble" gold. And for the next five hundred years, thousands of men throughout Europe spent much of their time laboring over glowing furnaces in smoke-filled laboratories, stirring bubbling pots, staring hopefully at boiling mixtures, and eagerly scanning odd old books in search of the secret of transmutation.

Some of the ideas of the Arabian alchemists apparently became garbled in the many translations made of their books. To some Europeans, Jabir's *al-iksar* became an "Elixir of Life"; a kind of magic potion that could make a person live forever or make the elderly young again. Others, correctly understanding that *al-iksar* meant a dry substance, thought Jabir had been talking about a magical sort of mineral or stone. In time, both these ideas became fixed in the beliefs of the European alchemists, and they thought there was both an "Elixir of Life" to be discovered, and a "Philosopher's Stone," which, if

Alchemists in the Middle Ages (above) and a reconstruction of a sixteenth-century alchemical laboratory (right).

they could discover how to make it, would enable them to turn any metal into gold. There was also still a great deal of magic and superstition mixed with alchemy, and many alchemists tried putting such things as "mole dust" and owl blood into their mineral mixtures, while others consulted astrological charts to see if the stars were in the proper position to give the best results to alchemical experiments. Many alchemists gained reputations as wizards and magicians because they surrounded their work with such mystery.

SORCERERS AND CHARLATANS

While most medieval alchemists were honest, sincere people with a belief in what they were doing, a good many men who called themselves alchemists were really just tricksters who would today be called "con men." They claimed to have found the secret of making gold by mixing and heating certain chemicals, and were more than willing to sell this "secret" to anyone foolish enough to pay a high price for it. They worked out many clever ways of fooling people into believing their claims. One way was to fill a hollow iron rod with powdered gold, plugging up the end of the rod with a bit of wax. The alchemist would offer to give a demonstration

A woodcut of a medieval alchemist in his laboratory

at the home of a noble or wealthy merchant, in which he would mix some liquids in a pot, heat them to boiling, and begin stirring them with the rod. The heat would melt the wax and the gold would suddenly flow out, appearing to everyone watching as if it had suddenly been formed out of the boiling liquid. The alchemist then would sell the recipe for the liquid mixture—and quickly leave.

Naturally, scams such as this soon gave alchemy and all alchemists a bad name. In 1317, Pope John XXII issued a decree against alchemists, and in 1380 the king of France passed a law forbidding anyone in his kingdom from studying alchemy. Most educated people felt that alchemists were either fakes or fools. Quite a few artists during the Middle Ages did paintings and woodcuts that made fun of alchemists, and a number of authors, including the famous Chaucer, wrote stories in which alchemists were comical characters.

Despite its bad reputation, the study of alchemy went on. Many alchemists *were* foolish people, and some were certainly frauds, but a good number were truly trying to learn new things, and it was some of those people who made discoveries and inventions that affected history. It was apparently a European alchemist who learned to mix charcoal, sulfur, and saltpeter together in a certain way, thus inventing gunpowder and changing the way wars were fought. European alchemists invented sulfuric acid, hydrochloric acid, and, probably, nitric acid, all of which are tremendously important in industry and science today. A European

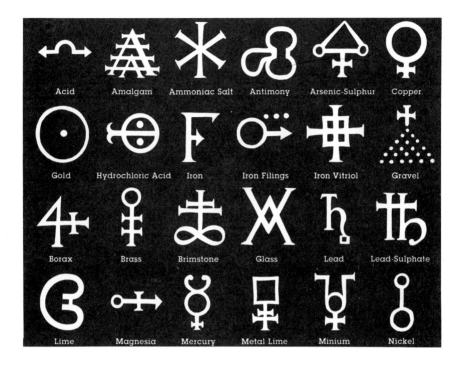

Alchemic symbols, including the one for hydrochloric acid, a chemical combination discovered by European alchemists

alchemist discovered how to make sugar from barley, and another, while distilling urine, discovered the element phosphorus.

THE FIRST
CHEMOTHERAPIST

In the 1500s, near the end of the Middle Ages, a number of doctors and scholars interested in medical problems began using alchemy to try to help cure diseases. These men were known as *iatrochemists*, or "healing chemists." The most famous of them was a Swiss known as Dr. Paracelsus. He had studied alchemy and shared the belief of most other alchemists that "base" metals could be turned into gold and that earth, air, fire, and water were the four elements of which everything was made, but he had also worked out a few new ideas of his own. He believed that a great many of the things that go on in a human body were caused by chemical action, and in this, of course, he was quite right. He also believed that alchemy shouldn't be used only to try to make gold and silver, but also to make marvelous remedies that could be used against disease. He felt that such medicines made from metals would be more effective than medicines made from plants, as most medicines then were, and he actually did cure a number of people's problems by giving them remedies made from mercury—which is still used in the treatment of certain diseases today. Thus, Paracelsus was actually the inventor of what is now known as *chemotherapy*, or treatment with chemicals.

A portrait of Paracelsus (1493–1541), the Swiss physician and "healing chemist" who invented chemotherapy

A lot of people, especially other doctors, disagreed with Paracelsus, but many others felt he was right and began to experiment with medicines made from mercury and other minerals. So even though Paracelsus had a number of wild ideas, he helped put alchemy on a path that led away from such things as trying to change lead into gold and trying to concoct elixirs of life, and made it more respectable.

Thus, by the end of the 1500s, a number of important discoveries and ideas had come from people who were interested in alchemy. But as to *understanding* why most of their discoveries and inventions had come about, the European alchemists of the Middle Ages were really no better off than the ancient Egyptian chemical workers of eighteen hundred years earlier. Most of them still believed in the four elements, in transmutation, and in the Philosopher's Stone. None of them knew what fire was or why iron rusted or why they sometimes got bad smells when they burned certain things. They generally just *accepted* whatever occurred.

But then something wonderful happened that brought about a great change!

A SCIENTIFIC REVOLUTION

What happened was that in the early 1600s there began a "revolution" that swept away all the old-fashioned ideas about alchemy and many other things, and created the new idea that we now call science. Men who were some of the world's first true scientists began to question many of the things that most alchemists had simply accepted. They began to think and experiment along new lines and made discoveries that helped build our world of today.

The scientific revolution actually had its beginnings in the mid-1500s. In 1543 a Polish astronomer known as Nicholas Copernicus published a book in which he showed that the earth went around the sun. This was an incredible, sensational new idea, because for thousands of years most everyone had believed without the slightest doubt that the earth was the center of the universe, and that the sun and stars went around *it*—after all, you could *see* them moving across the sky. But Copernicus provided the mathematical and logical proof that the earth was rushing through space in a vast, circular path around the sun, as were all the other planets, and that the stars were actually much farther away than people thought.

It took half a century for Copernicus's discovery to become accepted by most people, because there was a great deal of opposition to it, especially from Christian religious leaders who felt it was contrary to what was said in the Bible, and from scholars who refused to give up the old-fashioned beliefs they had grown up with. But for many people who were interested in such things as astronomy, chemistry, and medical research, Copernicus's discovery showed that established beliefs were not necessarily true just because they had been around for a long time. These people now started examining and picking apart such beliefs as the Philosopher's Stone, the four elements, and other ideas that had simply been accepted without the slightest doubt for hundreds of years. To do this, they took nothing for granted—they weighed, measured, experimented, observed, checked, and rechecked to find out if things *really* happened as alchemists for hundreds of years believed they did. In other words, these men began using what we now call the scientific method, and in doing so, they conceived the science of chemistry.

3

An Idea
Called Phlogiston

One of the first people to use scientific methods in chemistry was a wealthy Belgian nobleman by the name of Jan Baptista van Helmont. He was one of the first to argue against the old idea of earth, air, fire, and water as elements. Fire was not an element, he insisted; it was actually a one-of-a-kind thing that was a source of destruction for most substances. Earth wasn't an element either, said van Helmont—it was a substance that formed out of water. Van Helmont based this idea on the fact that many alchemists had found that when water was distilled over and over in a glass container, a small quantity of powdery stuff eventually formed—obviously, a kind of earth, said van Helmont. (He was wrong, of course, but it would be more than 150 years before anyone explained why this happened.)

Van Helmont was particularly interested in what happened to things when they burned, and in the early 1600s he performed a number of experiments to try to find out. One of his first experiments was quite simple; he weighed 62 pounds (28 kilograms) of charcoal, burned it until there was nothing left but ash, and then weighed the ash. He found that it weighed about one pound (.45 kilogram). Where had the other 61 pounds gone, he wondered.

He decided the 61 pounds had been changed by the burning into an invisible, formless vapor; this was more or less right. Inasmuch as he had discovered this new kind of substance, it was up to him to give it a name, so he decided to call it by the Greek word that meant "formless substance," which was "chaos." However, van Helmont used the Belgian pronunciation and spelling, and wrote the word as *gas*. He had, indeed, discovered the substance we now call by the name he gave it—gas.

By means of other experiments, van Helmont found there was a number of different kinds of gases—some odorless, some smelly, some poisonous, some explosive. Van Helmont's ideas and discoveries were accepted and respected by most other chemists of the 1600s, but for some reason the name he picked, gas, did not catch on right away. For

Jan Baptista van Helmont (1579–1644), a Flemish physician and chemist, discovered gas and challenged such long-standing beliefs as the four elements.

more than a hundred years after this time, most chemists simply called different kinds of gases "airs."

THE INVISIBLE SUBSTANCE

Van Helmont's discovery of gas was the first step toward knowing what happened when something burned. There were a lot of mysteries about the changes that took place when things were burned, and one of the most puzzling was what happened to most kinds of metals when they were "roasted," or calcined, by being heated in an open pot. They would change into different kinds of pitted, powdery substances that the alchemists had named *calx*, meaning "lime," because it looked like the material called lime that was left over when limestone was burned. According to the belief that all things were formed of earth, air, fire, and water, most alchemists believed that calx was just the left-over earth from which fire and the other elements had been removed. However, in the 1500s a number of alchemists had discovered that a calx always weighed *more* than the metal it came from. Naturally, this was a puzzle—a calx should have *lost* weight by having all the other elements taken out of it; how could it possibly have gained weight instead?

The reason for the increase in weight was, of course, that something had been *added* to the metal, not taken away. Under heat, oxygen from the air combines with metal to form a new substance (an oxide) that has the original weight of the metal plus the weight of the oxygen. Most alchemists couldn't have dreamed such a thing was possible, so they tried to explain the increase in weight with many kinds of imaginative ideas—such as that when a metal burned it got thicker.

FROM ALCHEMISTS
TO CHEMISTS

By the end of the 1600s there were still a good many alchemists in Europe still searching for the Philosopher's Stone so they could turn tin or lead into gold. But by this time there was also a number of men like Jan van Helmont, who called themselves chemists rather than alchemists and who studied substances and conducted experiments in order to learn about things and not simply to try to make themselves rich. Some of these men tried using scientific methods to find out why a calx weighed more than the metal it came from.

One of these men came fairly close to the truth. He was Jean Rey, a French doctor with a great interest in chemistry. Rey calcined some lead and tin in different ways, carefully watched what went on, and then tried to reason out what must have happened. In 1630 he wrote a little booklet that presented his ideas. He explained that when a metal was being calcined, the air around it became thicker and heavier from the heat, and some of this heavy air stuck to the metal, causing it to weigh more. Rey was off the mark as to what really happened, of course, but he was far closer than anyone else would be for 145 more years. However, few if any chemists seem to have accepted his explanation.

In 1669 one of the new chemists came up with a new idea of what combustion, or burning, actually was. He was a German named Johann Becher, and his idea was that solid substances that would burn, such as wood or a metal that could be calcined, were formed of three kinds of the element earth—a dry earth, a watery earth, and an oily earth. Burning, said Becher, was simply the oily earth flowing out of the solid. The heat also caused the watery earth to turn to steam, leaving only the dry earth as a powdery ash or as a calx. This idea satisfied a lot of chemists who still believed that earth was an element, but of course it still didn't explain why a calx was heavier than the metal it came from.

THE SKEPTICAL CHEMIST

At about the same time another of the new chemists was thinking about the calx mystery, and this was Robert Boyle, an Irishman, who was one of the best scientists of his time. In 1661, in a book he wrote called *The Sceptical Chymist*, Boyle cast scorn on the idea of earth, air, fire, and water as elements and brought forth the same idea that some of the ancient Greek scholars had—that all substances were formed of tiny particles. This was actually the beginning of our understanding of atoms today. Boyle attacked the calx mystery in 1673, and he did it by coming up with an idea that no other chemist (and of course, no alchemist) had apparently ever thought of—an idea that was typical of the scientific method.

Alchemists had nearly always done their calcining in open containers. Boyle thought of using a closed container to see if this would make a difference to either the formation of the calx or its weight. He weighed a piece of tin, put it in a glass container, sealed the container and heated it until he saw that a calx had formed on the tin. Then he broke open the container and weighed the calx-covered lump of tin. Of course, it weighed more than the original piece of tin had. To Boyle, this seemed to show that something had gotten into the sealed container and mixed with the calx, making it weigh more. But the only thing that had been done to the container, as far as Boyle could see, was that it had been heated over fire. Boyle decided that fire must have *weight*, and that particles of fire had passed through the glass of the container and soaked into the calx.

We can chuckle at such an idea now, but it was actually about the only possible answer Boyle could have arrived at, given the result of his experiment. However, Boyle had made a mistake. He had overlooked something that, if he had done it, would have made him think of a different answer. But it would be a hundred years before someone would correct his mistake. Meanwhile, because of Boyle's experiment, a good many chemists came to believe that fire had weight. Not all agreed with this, however.

Robert Boyle (1627–1691), a brilliant Irish scientist, argued that all substances were made up of tiny particles. His idea marked the beginning of our understanding of atoms.

A SUBSTANCE
CALLED PHLOGISTON

A number of years after Boyle's time, another of the new scientists began giving thought to the whole problem of what happened when things burned. His name was Georg Ernst Stahl, and he came up with the idea that most everyone felt sure was finally the right answer.

Stahl was a doctor who had been a teacher of chemistry at a German university and was still tremendously interested in chemistry even though he no longer taught it. In 1723 Stahl published a chemistry textbook in which he offered the idea that would be accepted by most chemists for the next seventy-five years—the idea known as *phlogiston*.

It seemed to Stahl that things burned because there was something *in* them that *allowed* them to burn, something that flowed out of them into the air as they were burning, and when it was all out, they could no longer burn. This was actually a little bit like Becher's "oily earth," idea, but Stahl called his mysterious substance *phlogiston*, from the Greek word meaning "flammable."

Stahl had done some experiments to check out his idea. He heated some of the metal zinc until it glowed cherry red, began to burn with a bright flame, then turned into a white calx. No matter how much this calx was heated it would never burn, Stahl found, and he believed this was simply because there was no phlogiston left in it. Next, Stahl burned some of the substance called phosphorus; it flamed brightly

Georg Ernst Stahl (1660–1734) pro-posed the theory that a mysterious substance, which he called phlogiston, *caused things to burn.*

and burned away, leaving an oily liquid which, like the calx of zinc, would not catch fire no matter how often flame was touched to it. Again, Stahl felt sure this was because all phlogiston had been removed from it.

But Stahl was a pretty good scientist and knew he needed more proof than this, so he thought up some more experiments to test the truth of what he now believed. It seemed to him that if he was right about phlogiston being taken out of things when they burned, it could also be put back into them and then they would change back into what they had been. So Stahl heated some calx of zinc to-gether with some charcoal (which Stahl thought must contain lots of phlogiston, because it would burn so well) and carefully watched what happened. Sure enough, as the charcoal burned, the calx turned back into zinc! To Stahl, this meant that as phlogiston left the charcoal it was soaked up by the calx, and together, the calx and phlogiston formed zinc. Stahl tried the same experiment using the acid of phosphorus and charcoal, and got the same result. The acid turned back into phosphorus.

What had happened, of course, was that a chemical reaction had taken place *removing* the oxygen from the zinc calx and the phosphorus acid, so that they had, indeed, returned to their original form. But to Stahl, what had happened was proof that his ideas about phlogiston were completely right.

Most other chemists, when they heard about Stahl's ideas and experiments, felt he had made a tremendous discovery. It looked as if the age-old mysteries about what burning was and about why some things would burn and others wouldn't, had been solved at last. Things burned because they had phlogiston in them, and burning itself was simply phlogiston coming out of things. It all seemed very logical. Stahl had even come up with a brand new—and perfectly correct—idea that the rusting of metals was actually a form of burning, and that rust was a calx. But he said that rusting was a much slower process than burning, with the metal giving off phlogiston so slowly that the flame of the burning couldn't even be seen. There was still the problem of why a calx of zinc or an acid of phosphorus weighed more than the original zinc or phosphorus from which they were made. Chemists finally came up with the rather odd idea that phlogiston must have "negative weight"—in other words, it weighed *less than nothing*, and so when it was gone out of a substance, the substance would actually weigh more. Many chemists were not very happy with this explanation, however.

The idea of phlogiston was almost completely accepted, and it influenced almost everything that chemists did for the next seventy-five years. If any new substance was discovered, its discoverer immediately had to determine whether or not it contained phlogiston.

UNCOVERING
THE ELEMENTS

In 1772, a number of European scientists—Daniel Rutherford of Scotland, Karl Scheele of Sweden, and Joseph Priestly and Henry Cavendish of England—made quantities of an "air" in which nothing would burn. A candle put into a jar full of this air would instantly go out. It was decided that this was because the air was so full of phlogiston that it just couldn't hold any more, and so it "blocked" the release of any phlogiston from a burning substance. It became known as "phlogisticated air." (What these men had done, in most cases, was to get rid of the oxygen and carbon dioxide in a quantity of air under a jar, leaving mostly nitrogen gas, which will not support combustion. Thus, they had actually all discovered nitrogen.)

*A reconstruction of the apparatus
used by Joseph Priestly in his
experiments on the composition of air*

In 1774, Joseph Priestly, who was an English Unitarian minister and an enthusiastic amateur chemist, discovered what he felt must be "*de*phlogisticated air" — air that had no phlogiston at all in it. Any glowing ember put into this air would immediately burst into flame, showing, it seemed to Priestly, that there was an enormous amount of room in this kind of air for lots and lots more phlogiston. (Priestly had actually isolated [separated from air] the gas oxygen that supports combustion. Oxygen had been discovered several years earlier by the Swedish chemist Karl Scheele, but Scheele didn't get a report of his discovery published until after Priestly did.)

Then, in 1776 came what seemed to be the crowning achievement. The Englishman Henry Cavendish, who was wealthy enough to be able to spend all his time just working at scientific projects and experiments, poured hydrochloric and sulfuric acids onto several different kinds of metals and collected the gas that was given off in a jar. If a candle or burning ember was put into the jar, the gas would burn with a flash of blue flame.

Cavendish called the gas "inflammable air," but he wondered if maybe it wasn't actually pure phlogiston. He thought that the acid made phlogiston come rushing out of the metal. (What Cavendish had actually done was to isolate the flammable gas we now call hydrogen.)

So, in the year Cavendish made his discovery, chemists could feel they had come a long way indeed from the days of the alchemists. They had made a great many new discoveries and they had scientific answers, based on facts, for many questions the alchemists had simply paid no attention to. They had taken the magic and mumbo-jumbo out of chemistry and made it a serious and sober search for knowledge.

But there were still some vexing problems. For one, no one still quite knew what to think about elements. Earth and fire had been ruled out as elements because it was generally believed that earth was formed out of water and that fire was simply the glow of heat. But no one was quite sure whether air and water were truly elements or not. There were a lot of questions about how certain substances, such as acids, were formed. And there was still that embarrassing question of why a calx weighed more than it should. Chemists still didn't know why many chemical changes took place as they did, and actually, chemistry was still nearly as "hit or miss" and uncertain as alchemy had been. Worst of all, it was headed down the wrong path, because it was based on the idea of phlogiston, which was completely wrong.

However, even as Priestly and Cavendish were making their discoveries and trying to fit them into the phlogiston idea, a French chemist was making the experiments and doing the thinking that was going to turn chemistry upside down and set it firmly on the right path. That chemist was Antoine Lavoisier.

4

Lavoisier Goes to Work

Antoine Laurent Lavoisier was born in Paris on August 26, 1743. His father and grandfather were both well-to-do lawyers, and the boy was reared to follow in their footsteps, so at the age of twenty he graduated from College Mazarin and entered the School of Law. But it was soon obvious to his family and friends that the young man was far more interested in science than in law, so his father tolerantly let him do what he wanted. Lavoisier began taking a course in chemistry, and by the time he was twenty-one he was even trying to become a member of the French Academy of Science — an organization of France's top scientists to which a person could only belong by being voted in by a majority of all the established members. Lavoisier was really too young to be a member and had no position as a scientist, but he began making careful scientific studies of a number of things and writing well-thought-out reports which he then sent to the

Antoine Lavoisier (1743–1794) as a young scientist. He would dedicate his life to the study and development of modern chemistry.

Academy in hopes of gaining the recognition he needed. Some of the reports he gave the Academy were on the cause of thunder; the cause of the aurora borealis (the "northern lights"); and the chemical makeup of the rock known as gypsum, from which plaster of paris is made. By the time he was twenty-five, Lavoisier's determination had paid off. He had impressed the members of the Academy enough so that he was admitted to the organization with the rank of "associate chemist."

He was still only a young beginning scientist, unknown to anyone outside Paris, but two years later his name became known to scientists throughout Europe. He gave the Academy a report on an experiment he had done which destroyed a belief then held by most chemists—the belief that water could be gradually turned into earth by being distilled over and over again. Over the past few hundred years a number of alchemists and chemists had apparently proved this by getting small amounts of powdery "earth" from water they distilled, but Lavoisier now showed that they had all been wrong.

OVERTURNING A POPULAR BELIEF

To distill a liquid, a chemist or alchemist poured a quantity of the liquid into a glass container and heated it over a fire. The liquid would boil and turn to steam which flowed out of the container through a long tube into another container—a cool one—where it would condense back into liquid. However, if there had been any solid substance dissolved in the liquid it would not, of course, turn to steam, but would be left behind in the heated container after all the liquid boiled away. Chemists and alchemists had found that when they distilled plain water with nothing dissolved in it, there was nevertheless almost always a solid left behind in the form of a thin, powdery film covering the bottom of the glass container. Everyone had always thought this was a kind of earth that had formed out of the water, and this was why most people still believed that water was an element which could form into earth, rock, wood, and other things.

But Lavoisier suspected that the "earth" wasn't really coming out of the distilled water at all, and to prove it he did something that no other chemist or alchemist had ever thought of doing. First, he carefully cleaned and weighed a glass container of the kind called a *pelican*. Into this he put a quantity of the purest water he could find, and he then weighed the container and water together, so that he now knew the separate weights of both the container and the water. Then he began to distill and re-distill the water. (The pelican was especially designed for doing this; in a dome at its top the steam condensed back into water which then trickled through tubes that curved back and emptied into the pelican's bottom, so that the water began boiling again.) Lavoisier kept this up for 101 days, at the end of which a quantity of powdery "earth" had apparently formed in the bottom of the pelican. He removed the water and the powder and weighed them both. Then he cleaned and dried the pelican and weighed it. He found that the pelican now weighed slightly *less* than it had when he had begun his experiment. However, the weight of the powdery substance was just about the amount of the weight that had been lost by the pelican.

What had happened was obvious. The powdery stuff hadn't come out of the water at all; it had come from the pelican! It was formed of tiny bits of glass that had crumbled off because of the steady heat and the action of the boiling water pounding against the glass. Thus, Lavoisier had now proved that water *didn't* form earth while it was being distilled. Any other chemist or alchemist during the past hundreds of years could have done what Lavoisier did, which was simply to *weigh* everything, but he was the only one who had thought of doing it — the only one to *really* use the scientific way of doing things. Suddenly, he was famous!

THE NOBLE CHEMIST

In 1771, Lavoisier married Marie Anne Pierrette Paulze, who almost at once began training herself to become his scientific assistant. The marriage was to be a long and happy one. In 1772, Lavoisier's father bought his son a "title," making the young chemist a member of the French nobility or ruling class. This would turn out to be a serious mistake.

In the same year he became a noble, Lavoisier began working on the old baffling problem of why the calxes of substances that had been calcined were

heavier than the original substances. He had thought about this for a long time, and had come to the conclusion that air must have something to do with it. He thought that perhaps air was being absorbed by a substance as it was calcined, making it heavier.

Lavoisier began a long series of experiments. He weighed a quantity of phosphorus and then heated it in a closed container until it burned and turned into a whitish powder (in an open container it would have become a liquid). Weighing the powder, he found that it of course weighed more than the phosphorus had. Obviously something had been added to it to make it weigh more. When Robert Boyle had done this same sort of experiment about a hundred years earlier, he had thought that the fire had weight, and that particles of fire were passing through the glass of the container and soaking into the calx to give it more weight, but Lavoisier did not believe that anything could have gotten into the container from outside. He believed that whatever had given the calx the extra weight must have been inside the container. But there had been nothing in the container but the phosphorus—and air. To Lavoisier, there seemed no doubt that as the phos-

A reproduction of a painting
by Jacques Louis David
of Lavoisier and his wife,
Marie Anne, who was also his
scientific assistant

phorus burned it absorbed air that went into the powder that formed. Air has weight, of course, and this was what had made the difference, he felt.

He did the experiment again, using sulfur. The result was the same. The burned sulfur weighed more than the sulfur he had started with, and it appeared to him that it had absorbed a large amount of air.

Lavoisier thought this over and decided that if air *was* mixed into the substances left over after something was calcined, the air would have to be *released* by those substances when they were turned back into their original form. He had to find out if this was correct, so he prepared another experiment, using special equipment.

He took some red lead (the calx formed by burning lead) and heated it together with some charcoal in an iron container. A tube led out of the container into another container half-filled with water in which a long glass jar was suspended upside-down. A slender pipe ran from the tube up inside the jar, which was about two-thirds full of water. Thus, if Lavoisier was right, and air was given off by the red lead as it turned back into lead, that air would flow down the tube and up the pipe, and it would push the water down out of the glass jar, making the water in the other container rise.

And that was exactly what happened. But Lavoisier was astounded to see that as the red lead turned back into metal, it gave off an amount of air that seemed to him to be at least a thousand times greater than the entire amount of red lead.

He removed a large quantity of this air from the top of the jar where it had collected and tested it in several ways. He decided that it was actually something that was mixed into the whole air, and he called it "an elastic fluid," meaning it could stretch or shrink to fill any space. He believed this substance was what made it possible for things to be calcined, and that when all "elastic fluid" was gone out of the air that was around a substance being calcined, the calcination would stop.

WEIGHING
THE EVIDENCE

Because he had gotten this "elastic fluid" out of a metal calx, Lavoisier now felt sure that what was true of calxes of nonmetal substances, such as sulfur and phosphorus, must be true of metal calxes as well—they gained their weight from the air they were calcined in, and not in any other way. To prove this, Lavoisier did the same experiment with some tin and lead. He weighed bits of these metals and put them into containers which he then sealed tight so that nothing could possibly get into them. He weighed the containers and heated them until the bits of metal in each formed a calx. He weighed the containers again, establishing that their weights were still exactly the same. When he opened them, he noticed that a small amount of air rushed into each, indicating that some of the air that had been inside had *gone* somewhere, leaving room for new air to take its place. When he weighed the calxes he of course found that they were heavier than the metals had been. They could only have gained that weight from the air that had been inside the containers, Lavoisier felt sure, and that was where the missing air had gone!

This experiment was actually the same as the experiment Robert Boyle had done, but with one big difference—Boyle had not thought to weigh the *sealed* container as Lavoisier had. By weighing the sealed containers before and after the calcining, and finding that the weight was the same, Lavoisier proved that nothing had gotten into the containers. Of course, this destroyed Boyle's idea about "fire particles" going through the glass sides of the container and mixing with a calx to give it extra weight, for that would have added extra weight to the closed container. But even more important, the result of these experiments convinced Lavoisier that air was involved when anything was calcined, and he was beginning to suspect that air must be involved in *any* kind of burning. Thus, he was well on the way to putting together the ideas that would be the basis for our modern understanding of *combustion*.

DISCOVERING THE PROPERTIES OF AIR

Shortly after this, the Academy of Science asked Lavoisier to help check the work of two French chemists who had done an experiment which, they claimed, had produced a surprising result. The two had calcined some mercury to get the powdery red calx that came from burned mercury, and had then heated the calx as hot as they could make it, to see what would happen. What had happened, they said, was that the calx had turned back into mercury! This had astounded the two, and it astounded every other chemist who heard about it, because it seemed to be impossible. Everyone knew that you could make a calx of mercury turn back into mercury if you heated it together with charcoal, but they thought that was because phlogiston from the charcoal flowed into the calx. However, there hadn't been any charcoal with the calx when the two men heated it, so where could the phlogiston have come from?

Lavoisier carefully repeated their experiment, but he put in some special touches of his own that would help him determine some additional facts. He calcined some mercury in a sealed container until he got enough of the red calx to use, and then he checked the air that was left in the container. A measurement showed there was one-sixth less of it, and when he put a mouse and a candle into it, the mouse immediately died and the candle instantly went out.

Lavoisier then proceeded to heat the red calx by itself as the other two said they had done. Watching carefully, he saw that as the calx got hotter its color got redder. When the container he was heating the calx in was nearly red-hot itself, Lavoisier saw the red calx slowly disappear and a silvery blob of mercury take its place.

He had proved that the other two chemists had been correct, but now he kept on going to see what he could find out for himself. He tested the air that was left over from this experiment and found that a burning candle put into it began to burn with a brighter flame, while a piece of red glowing charcoal burst into flame and burned with such brilliance that, said Lavoisier, "the eyes could hardly stand it." Furthermore, he found that small animals could breathe this air very nicely.

As was his way, Lavoisier now thought long and carefully about the possible meaning of the facts these experiments had revealed. The air that was released by a calx when it turned back into its original form helped things burn better and seemed to make breathing easier, so Lavoisier thought of it as "highly breathable air." But the air that was left over when something was burned to form a calx would not let things burn and could not be breathed. It seemed clear that when a substance was calcined it absorbed "highly breathable air," leaving behind only the poisonous air. This meant that the ordinary air people breathed every day, which was the air a chemist started with when he calcined anything, was a *mixture* of "highly breathable air" and poisonous air.

When Lavoisier realized this, he accomplished two things. He had discovered that air was a mixture of things rather than a single thing, and he had thereby destroyed the two-thousand-year-old belief that air was an element, for an element cannot be a mixture.

It was just about at this time, in the year 1775, that Joseph Priestly, the Englishman, produced his "dephlogisticated air," and when Lavoisier heard of this he realized that "dephlogisticated air" was the same as what he was calling "highly breathable air." Priestly was calling it "dephlogisticated air" because, like most chemists, he still believed in phlogiston, but Lavoisier now knew that the whole idea of phlogiston was wrong. A calx wasn't formed by phlogiston coming out of a burning substance, it was formed by something in the air going in!

5

The Creation of Modern Chemistry

In the early spring of 1775, Lavoisier told of his discovery in an article he wrote for a little French scientific magazine. He entitled the article, "On the Nature of the Principle that Combines with Metals During Their Calcination and Increases Their Weight." He explained that what he meant by "the Principle," was "the purest and most healthful part of the air" (actually, the gas we now call oxygen). His article stated that things burned because this part of the air went into them, and it was the additional weight of this part of the air that made a calx weigh more than the metal it was formed from. All this was completely contrary to the whole idea of phlogiston, so Lavoisier was actually *attacking* that idea, although he didn't come right out and say so.

But apparently most other chemists didn't hear about Lavoisier's article and the new ideas it presented. They continued to believe wholeheartedly in phlogiston. In 1777, Karl Scheele, the Swede who was the actual discoverer of oxygen, published a report that showed he had formed some of the same ideas as Lavoisier, but still believed in phlogiston anyway. Scheele had been experimenting with the gases oxygen and nitrogen, and he had come to the conclusion that they were two separate things that helped form the air that people breathed. But Scheele called oxygen "fire air," and nitrogen "foul air," and said that things would burn in "fire air" because it was able to soak up the phlogiston they gave off as they burned, whereas nothing would burn in "foul air" because it was so loaded with phlogiston that it couldn't soak up any more. Unlike Lavoisier, Scheele was still so completely convinced of the phlogiston idea that he was trying to make it fit into everything he did.

AN IMPORTANT YEAR

In 1778, Lavoisier made a few changes in the article he had written in 1775 and gave it to the French Academy of Science. The article was published in the Academy's official magazine, which was read by a great many scientists throughout Europe. Most of these men now realized that Lavoisier was attacking the whole idea of phlogiston, and that if he was right, he had discovered an entirely new system of chemistry. His ideas became known as "anti-phlogistic chemistry" (meaning "against phlogiston"), and they caused tremendous argument. While some scientists decided that Lavoisier was completely right, many others bitterly attacked his ideas, refusing to give up their belief in phlogiston.

It was also in the year 1778 that Lavoisier made the announcement that breathing is a form of combustion. Experimenting with birds and small animals, he let them breathe pure oxygen and found that they exhaled, or breathed out, carbon dioxide, which was then called "fixed air." From this, he decided that the oxygen burned carbon in a creature's body, producing the carbon dioxide and causing the heat that keeps a body warm. This was a tremendously important discovery to doctors and scientists doing medical research, because it explained why blood carries oxygen to every cell in a creature's body—so it can be burned for the energy that keeps the body alive.

DISCOVERING THE PROPERTIES OF WATER

In 1781, Joseph Priestly did an experiment that had a surprising result. He mixed together in a container a quantity of the "dephlogisticated air" (oxygen) he had discovered in 1774, and a quantity of the "inflammable air" (hydrogen) that Henry Cavendish had produced in 1776, and shot an electric spark into the mixture. To his astonishment, a quantity of colorless liquid formed, and when Priestly tested this, he found that it was water! Cavendish heard of this experiment and tried it for himself, with the same result. Trying to make the phlogiston idea fit what had happened, Cavendish finally decided that "inflammable air" must be a combination of phlogiston and water, and that the electric spark had made the phlogiston flow out of it, leaving the water behind.

But when Lavoisier heard of these experiments he had a good idea of what had really happened. He performed the same experiment, thought over the results, and then, in 1783, made an announcement in which he explained what had taken place. He stated that water, which was still believed by some scientists to be an element, was actually a *compound*. It was formed of the two substances that had been used in the experiment—Cavendish's "inflammable air," which Lavoisier now named "hydrogen" (from two Greek words meaning "water maker") and Priestly's "dephlogisticated air," which Lavoisier had named "oxygen" (from Greek words that mean "acid maker"). Lavoisier also now called these two substances "gases" rather than "airs" (although, when he wrote the word, he spelled it "gaz").

This announcement was like a bomb explosion! With it, Lavoisier had destroyed the old idea that water was an element; had shown once again that phlogiston really didn't exist; had supplied useful, descriptive names for two substances that were called many different things; and had re-introduced the useful word "gas," which van Helmont had introduced more than 150 years before, but which had seldom if ever been used. It was a big step for chemistry!

This nineteenth-century French wood engraving shows Lavoisier in his laboratory, determining that water was not an element but a compound composed of hydrogen and oxygen.

In 1785 Lavoisier performed an experiment that added more proof to his declaration that water was formed from hydrogen and oxygen. In this experiment, water was squirted down a cannon barrel that had been heated red hot. The water instantly vaporized into steam, of course, and the steam was collected in a container at the end of the barrel. Lavoisier then separated it into oxygen and hydrogen. Hydrogen gas that was manufactured in this way was used to fill giant balloons that made the world's first air flights at that time.

A year later Lavoisier published an "official" attack on the whole phlogiston idea in which, for the first time, he came right out and said that phlogiston just didn't exist. He showed that while the idea of phlogiston seemed to logically explain what was happening when things burned, it was totally wrong because it stated that the source of fire was *inside* the thing that was burning, whereas as he had shown, the source of the fire was actually the gas oxygen, which was in the air.

At this point, a good many chemists became convinced that Lavoisier was right about everything, and they threw away the idea of phlogiston and began to think in terms of oxygen, hydrogen, and the rest of Lavoisier's ideas. They called burning *oxidation*, to show that, as Lavoisier had insisted, it was caused by oxygen going into things. With many scientists taking on these ideas of Lavoisier's, modern chemistry — *our* way of thinking about combustion, elements, and other aspects of chemistry — came into being.

OLD IDEAS DIE HARD

But not everyone gave up phlogiston immediately and came around to Lavoisier's way of thinking. A number of chemists grimly hung on to the old ideas. Priestly never quite gave up phlogiston, and Cavendish hedged by saying that phlogiston explained most things just as well as the oxidation idea did. Many of the older French and German chemists also refused to believe there was no such thing as phlogiston. And a few chemists even came up with completely new ideas that challenged Lavoisier, such as that it was hydrogen, and not oxygen, that was the cause of burning. But in time, all these ideas finally died away and Lavoisier's modern chemistry was left—because, as everyone could see, it was *right*.

A NEW NOMENCLATURE

The new chemistry needed new names for many things because the old names—such as "calx," "fixed air," and so on—were now meaningless. So in 1787, Lavoisier and a number of French chemists who had eagerly accepted the new chemistry, put together a book called *The Method of Chemical Nomenclature* (naming), in which they provided new names for most of the substances then known. These names, which were mostly created by Lavoisier, were designed to show exactly what each substance was formed of, so that instead of being a "calx of tin," or a "calx of lead," these substances became "tin oxide," and "lead oxide," to show that the metal was in combination with oxygen. The substances that alchemists and chemists had called "salts," which were formed by the action of acids, were renamed to show what acid they were formed from—"sulphates" from sulfuric acid, "nitrates" from nitric acid, and so on. Nearly all these names that were created by Lavoisier are the same ones used today.

The Method of Chemical Nomenclature also contained a list of what Lavoisier and other French chemists believed to be the true elements, substances that could not be broken down into something else. The list included oxygen, hydrogen, sulfur, phosphorus, and many other substances that we now know to be true elements, but it also contained a few things that are *not* elements, such as light and chalk. It also left out a good many things that have since been found to be elements. However, despite the mistakes and omissions, Lavoisier's list was the final end of the ancient earth-air-fire-water theory of elements, and the beginning of the modern idea of elements as we understand them today.

THE FIRST
CHEMISTRY TEXTBOOK

Lavoisier had also been working on another book, which was published in 1789. It was titled *Elementary Book of Chemistry*, and in it Lavoisier presented his ideas on what the new chemistry should do. He suggested that the chief purpose of chemistry was to discover the composition or makeup of every substance that is found in nature, and this could only be done by breaking a substance down into its elements (analyzing it), and then reproducing it by recombining its elements (synthesizing it). Lavoisier also presented an idea that scientists call "The Law of Conservation of Matter" — that no substance can either be created or destroyed, but can only be *changed*, either by nature or in a laboratory process. Thus, said Lavoisier, no matter what seemed to happen in an experiment, there was still the same

```
                                      Ti = 50     Zr = 90      ? = 180

                                      V = 51      Nb = 94      Ta = 182

                                      Cr = 52     Mo = 96      W = 186

H = 1                                 Mn = 55     Rh = 104, 4  Pt = 197, 4

    Be =  9, 4  Mg = 24               Fe = 56     Ru = 104, 4  Ir = 198

      B = 11    Al = 27, 4  Ni = Co = 59          Pd = 106, 6  Os = 199

      C = 12    Si = 28               Cu = 63, 4  Ag = 108     Hg = 200

      N = 14    P = 31                Zn = 65, 2  Cd = 112

      O = 16    S = 32                 ? = 68     Ur = 116     Au = 197?

      F = 19    Cl = 35, 5             ? = 70     Sn = 118

Li = 7  Na = 23    K = 39            As = 75      Sb = 122     Bi = 210?

                  Ca = 40            Se = 79, 4   Te = 128?

                   ? = 45            Br = 80       J = 127

                  ?Er = 56           Rb = 85, 4   Cs = 133     Tl = 204

                  ?Yt = 60           Sr = 87, 6   Ba = 137     Pb = 207

                  ?In = 75, 6        Ce = 92

                                     La = 94

                                     Di = 95

                                     Th = 118?
```

Above: From a page in the Journal of the Russian Chemical Society *(St. Petersburg, 1869) showing Dmitri Mendeleev's (1834–1907) table of elements based on their properties and the order of their atomic weights. Mendeleev predicted new elements would be discovered to fill gaps in his table.*

PERIODIC TABLE

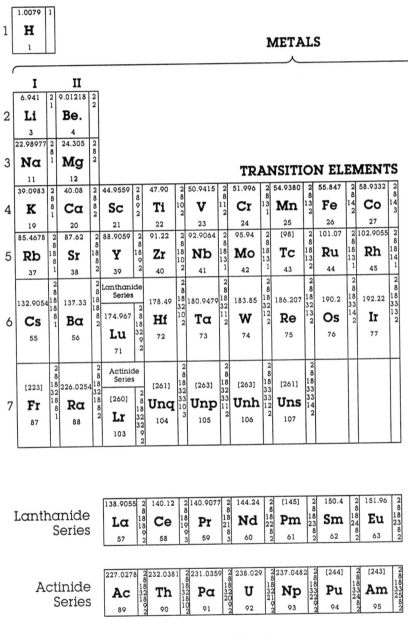

METALS

TRANSITION ELEMENTS

	I	II
1	1.0079 / 1 **H** 1	
2	6.941 / 2,1 **Li** 3	9.01218 / 2,2 **Be.** 4
3	22.98977 / 2,8,1 **Na** 11	24.305 / 2,8,2 **Mg** 12

	I	II							
4	39.0983 / 2,8,8,1 **K** 19	40.08 / 2,8,8,2 **Ca** 20	44.9559 / 2,8,9,2 **Sc** 21	47.90 / 2,8,10,2 **Ti** 22	50.9415 / 2,8,11,2 **V** 23	51.996 / 2,8,13,1 **Cr** 24	54.9380 / 2,8,13,2 **Mn** 25	55.847 / 2,8,14,2 **Fe** 26	58.9332 / 2,8,14,3 **Co** 27
5	85.4678 / 2,8,18,8,1 **Rb** 37	87.62 / 2,8,18,8,2 **Sr** 38	88.9059 / 2,8,18,9,2 **Y** 39	91.22 / 2,8,18,10,2 **Zr** 40	92.9064 / 2,8,18,13,1 **Nb** 41	95.94 / 2,8,18,13,1 **Mo** 42	[98] / 2,8,18,13,1 **Tc** 43	101.07 / 2,8,18,13,2 **Ru** 44	102.9055 / 2,8,18,14,1 **Rh** 45
6	132.9054 / 2,8,18,18,8,1 **Cs** 55	137.33 / 2,8,18,18,8,1 **Ba** 56	Lanthanide Series / 2,8,18,18,2 — 174.967 / 2,8,18,32,8,9,2 **Lu** 71	178.49 / 2,8,18,32,10,2 **Hf** 72	180.9479 / 2,8,18,32,11,2 **Ta** 73	183.85 / 2,8,18,32,12,2 **W** 74	186.207 / 2,8,18,32,13,2 **Re** 75	190.2 / 2,8,18,32,14,2 **Os** 76	192.22 / 2,8,18,32,13,2 **Ir** 77
7	[223] / 2,8,18,32,18,8,1 **Fr** 87	226.0254 / 2,8,18,32,18,8,2 **Ra** 88	Actinide Series / 2,8,18,32,18,8,2 — [260] / 2,8,18,32,32,9,2 **Lr** 103	[261] / 2,8,18,32,10,2 **Unq** 104	[263] / 2,8,18,32,32,11,2 **Unp** 105	[263] / 2,8,18,32,33,12,2 **Unh** 106	[261] / 2,8,18,32,33,14,2 **Uns** 107		

Lanthanide Series

138.9055 / 2,8,18,18,9,2 **La** 57	140.12 / 2,8,18,19,9,2 **Ce** 58	140.9077 / 2,8,18,21,8,2 **Pr** 59	144.24 / 2,8,18,22,8,2 **Nd** 60	[145] / 2,8,18,23,8,2 **Pm** 61	150.4 / 2,8,18,24,8,2 **Sm** 62	151.96 / 2,8,18,23,8,2 **Eu** 63

Actinide Series

227.0278 / 2,8,18,32,18,9,2 **Ac** 89	232.0381 / 2,8,18,32,18,10,2 **Th** 90	231.0359 / 2,8,18,32,20,9,2 **Pa** 91	238.029 / 2,8,18,32,21,9,2 **U** 92	237.0482 / 2,8,18,32,22,9,2 **Np** 93	[244] / 2,8,18,32,24,8,2 **Pu** 94	[243] / 2,8,18,32,25,8,2 **Am** 95

A modern periodic table of the elements.

OF THE ELEMENTS

Noble gases

NONMETALS

	III	IV	V	VI	VII	VIII
						4.00260 2
						He
						2
	10.81 2,3	12.011 2,4	14.0067 2,5	15.9994 2,6	18.998403 2,7	20.179 2,8
	B	**C**	**N**	**O**	**F**	**Ne**
	5	6	7	8	9	10
	26.98154 2,8,3	28.0855 2,8,4	30.97376 2,8,5	32.06 2,8,6	35.453 2,8,7	39.948 2,8,8
	Al	**Si**	**P**	**S**	**Cl**	**Ar**
	13	14	15	16	17	18
58.70 2,8,16,2	63.546 2,8,18,1	65.38 2,8,18,2	69.72 2,8,18,3	72.59 2,8,18,4	74.9216 2,8,18,5	78.96 2,8,18,6	79.904 2,8,18,7	83.80 2,8,18,8
Ni	**Cu**	**Zn**	**Ga**	**Ge**	**As**	**Se**	**Br**	**Kr**
28	29	30	31	32	33	34	35	36
106.4 2,8,18,18,0	107.868 2,8,18,18,1	112.41 2,8,18,18,2	114.82 2,8,18,18,3	118.69 2,8,18,18,4	121.75 2,8,18,18,5	127.60 2,8,18,18,6	126.9045 2,8,18,18,7	131.30 2,8,18,18,8
Pd	**Ag**	**Cd**	**In**	**Sn**	**Sb**	**Te**	**I**	**Xe**
46	47	48	49	50	51	52	53	54
195.09 2,8,18,32,17,1	196.9665 2,8,18,32,18,1	200.59 2,8,18,32,18,2	204.37 2,8,18,32,18,3	207.2 2,8,18,32,18,4	208.9804 2,8,18,32,18,5	[209] 2,8,18,32,18,6	[210] 2,8,18,32,18,7	[222] 2,8,18,32,18,8
Pt	**Au**	**Hg**	**Tl**	**Pb**	**Bi**	**Po**	**At**	**Rn**
78	79	80	81	82	83	84	85	86

RARE EARTH ELEMENTS

157.25 2,8,18,23,9,2	158.9254 2,8,18,27,8,2	162.50 2,8,18,28,8,2	164.9304 2,8,18,29,8,2	167.26 2,8,18,30,8,2	168.9342 2,8,18,31,8,2	173.04 2,8,18,32,8,2
Gd	**Tb**	**Dy**	**Ho**	**Er**	**Tm**	**Yb**
64	65	66	67	68	69	70

[247] 2,8,18,32,23,9,2	[247] 2,8,18,32,26,9,2	[251] 2,8,10,32,28,8,2	[254] 2,8,18,32,29,8,2	[257] 2,8,18,32,30,8,2	[258] 2,8,18,32,31,8,2	[259] 2,8,18,32,32,8,2
Cm	**Bk**	**Cf**	**Es**	**Fm**	**Md**	**No**
96	97	98	99	100	101	102

amount of substances (matter) left at the end of the experiment as there had been in the beginning. This could be shown by weighing everything at the beginning of an experiment and at its completion, as Lavoisier had always done. The book also contained a great deal of information on experiments and ideas of Lavoisier and other French chemists, and a new list of thirty-three elements (somewhat different from the list in the other book), twenty of which are recognized as true elements today. The book was actually the first modern chemistry textbook ever written.

DEATH OF THE NOBLE CHEMIST

If Antoine Lavoisier had lived anywhere but in France, he might have lived on for a good many years and done a great deal more important work in chemistry. But in 1789 France entered a long period of violent disorder, bloodshed, and warfare known as the French Revolution. The French people revolted against the king and the nobles, killing most of those that weren't able to escape from the country. And Lavoisier was a noble. Despite his fame as a scientist, despite the number of useful things he had done for his country, and despite the fact that he was a liberal and was actually in favor of the revolution, he was executed on May 8, 1794, on the guillotine. When another famous French scientist heard of this he exclaimed, "It only took them an instant to cut off that head, but there may not be another one like it in a hundred years!"

An illustration depicting Lavoisier being apprehended in his laboratory. He was arrested and brought to trial in 1794 for being a noble.

This wasn't far from the truth. Antoine Lavoisier was the sort of person who stands out from most others; he had a brilliant mind that was able to fit facts together to produce a clear picture. He did not make any startling discoveries of new substances as Priestly and Cavendish did, and he didn't invent any useful new equipment as many chemists did. What he did was simply to check very carefully every detail of an experiment and logically think over the facts the experiment presented, so that he was able to figure out exactly what had happened. In this way he destroyed the incorrect idea of phlogiston and ended once and for all the old, old belief that earth, air, fire, and water were the basic elements from which all other things were formed. By wiping out those wrong ideas, by supplying the knowledge of how oxygen caused combustion, and by providing an understanding of what the real elements are, Antoine Lavoisier literally created the modern science of chemistry.

LAVOISIER'S LEGACY

By the time of his death, Lavoisier's ideas had spread to all parts of Europe as well as to America, and many chemists were doing things as he had done them and thinking about things in the same ways he had thought about them. In 1797 some experiments by a Russian chemist, Vasily Petrov, helped to prove further that combustion was caused by oxygen, and that the old phlogiston idea, to which a few chemists were still clinging, was completely wrong. In 1802, John Dalton, an Englishman who wholeheartedly believed in Lavoisier's ideas and methods, carried the new chemistry a step further when he came up with the idea that all matter was formed of "elementary particles" or atoms, and that different elements were made up of different atoms. Robert Boyle had suggested this about 140 years earlier, but Dalton's atomic theory was based on a great deal of careful work, and it was the scientific basis for our present-day understanding of atoms.

In 1807, another Englishman, Humphrey Davy, following Lavoisier's urging to break everything down into its elements, discovered two new elements, sodium and potassium, when he broke down the substances known as soda and potash. Davy went on to discover the elements barium, boron, calcium, magnesium, silicon, and strontium, adding to the list of elements that Lavoisier had produced. He also showed that some of the substances Lavoisier had thought were elements were actually compounds that could be broken down.

By the end of the first quarter of the nineteenth century, the new chemistry developed by Antoine Lavoisier was firmly established, and the idea of phlogiston was dead and buried forever. Every person who has worked in chemistry since has done so on the basis of facts and knowledge provided by Antoine Lavoisier, the father of modern chemistry.

Glossary

Alchemy. The name given to a combination of chemistry, "magic," and philosophical ideas practiced by many people of Europe and the Near East during the Middle Ages. The main purpose of alchemy was to try to find a means of turning a common metal such as lead into gold.

Al-iksar. An Arabic term meaning "dry material," which was changed to "elixir" in Europe, as the name for a magical potion.

Calcine. To burn something until nothing remains of it but ashes or a powder.

Calx. The old-fashioned name for the substance left after a mineral, such as a metal, has been burned or roasted. We now generally call this substance an oxide.

Chemotherapy. The treatment of a disease or health disorder by means of a chemical substance that can kill or check the disease or condition.

Combustion. Any form of burning, which is the chemical union of oxygen with another substance.

Compound. A substance formed of two or more different kinds of atoms of different elements, which can therefore be broken down into two or more different substances. For example, lead oxide, formed of lead and oxygen, can be broken down into the metal lead and the gas oxygen.

Distill. To purify a liquid by heating it until it turns into steam, then cooling the steam until it becomes a liquid again. When the steam is formed, any impurities in the liquid, such as dissolved solids, will be left behind, and the liquid condensed from the steam will therefore be absolutely pure.

Element. A substance composed of only one kind of atom, which therefore cannot be broken down into different substances as a compound can. The element iron is formed of only iron atoms and cannot be broken down into anything else.

Fuse. To mix together two or more substances, such as metals, by melting them together to form a liquid which, when cooled and hardened, will be a single substance. Tin and copper can be fused together to form the metal known as bronze.

Gas. The vaporous form of matter (see *matter*).

Iatrochemists. A group of medieval scholars who believed that alchemy should be used for healing.

Matter. Substances that occupy space and form the physical universe. The three forms of matter visible to humans are solids, liquids, and gases. A fourth form, known as plasma, consists of electrically charged atoms of gas present inside stars.

Oxidation. The combination of the element oxygen with another element or compound, resulting in the chemical activity called burning or combustion.

Phlogiston. The name, meaning "flammable," given to what was once believed to be a substance present in many things which caused them to be able to burn.

Sublimate. To turn a solid into a gas by means of heat. When the gas is cooled into a liquid it has different chemical properties (characteristics) from the solid.

Transmutation. The changing of an element into a different element. Medieval alchemists tried unsuccessfully to transmute lead into gold; however, transmutation does take place naturally as a radioactive element such as uranium alters its atomic structure and becomes first radium, then polonium, then lead.

For Further Reading

Chisolm, Jane, and Johnson, Mary. *Introduction to Chemistry*. Tulsa: Usborne-Hayes, 1983.

Gallant, Roy. *Exploring Chemistry*. New York: Doubleday, 1958.

Grey, Vivian. *The Chemist Who Lost His Head: The Story of Antoine Lavoisier*. New York: Coward McCann, 1982.

Irwin, Keith Gordon. *The Romance of Chemistry: From Ancient Alchemy to Nuclear Fission*. New York: Viking, 1959.

Kenny, Hugh, and Newcome, Ellsworth. *Alchemy to Atoms*. New York: Putnam, 1961.

Kramer, Stephen P. *How to Think Like a Scientist: Answering Questions by the Scientific Method*. New York: Crowell, 1987.

Marcus, Rebecca B. *Antoine Lavoisier and the Revolution in Chemistry*. New York: Watts, 1964.

Rosen, Sidney, *Dr. Paracelsus*. Boston: Little, Brown, 1959.

Index